my itty-bitty bio

Mary Anning

Published in the United States of America by Cherry Lake Publishing
Ann Arbor, Michigan
www.cherrylakepublishing.com

Content Adviser: Jessica Criales, Doctoral Candidate, History Department, Rutgers University
Reading Adviser: Marla Conn MS, Ed., Literacy specialist, Read-Ability, Inc.
Book Design: Jennifer Wahi
Illustrator: Jeff Bane

Photo Credits: ©ian woolcock/Shutterstock, 5; ©lafoto/Shutterstock, 7; ©Dorling Kindersley/Thinkstock, 9; ©SAQ/Shutterstock, 11, 22; ©frantic 00/Shutterstock, 13, 23; ©sarkao/Shutterstock, 15; ©lcrms/Shutterstock, 17; ©PD-1923, 19; ©Paul Fearn / Alamy Stock Photo, 21; Cover, 10, 12, 18, Jeff Bane; Various frames throughout, ©Shutterstock Images

Library of Congress Cataloging-in-Publication Data

Names: Spiller, Sara, author. | Bane, Jeff, 1957- illustrator.
Title: Mary Anning / by Sara Spiller ; [illustrator, Jeff Bane].
Other titles: My itty-bitty bio.
Description: Ann Arbor, MI : Cherry Lake Publishing, [2018] | Series: My itty-bitty bio | Includes index.
Identifiers: LCCN 2018003111| ISBN 9781534128842 (hardcover) | ISBN 9781534132047 (pbk.) | ISBN 9781534130548 (pdf) | ISBN 9781534133747 (hosted ebook)
Subjects: LCSH: Anning, Mary, 1799-1847--Juvenile literature. | Women paleontologists--England--Biography--Juvenile literature. | Paleontologists--England--Biography--Juvenile literature. | Ichthyosaurus--Juvenile literature. | Fossils--Juvenile literature.
Classification: LCC QE707.A56 S674 2018 | DDC 560/.92 [B] --dc23
LC record available at https://lccn.loc.gov/2018003111

Printed in the United States of America
Corporate Graphics

table of contents

About the author: Sara Spiller is a native of the state of Michigan. She enjoys reading comic books and hanging out with her cats. She wants to help empower people all over the world, including women who study fossils.

About the illustrator: Jeff Bane and his two business partners own a studio along the American River in Folsom, California, home of the 1849 Gold Rush. When Jeff's not sketching or illustrating for clients, he's either swimming or kayaking in the river to relax.

my story

I was born in England in 1799. I had an older brother. His name was Joseph.

I was hit by **lightning** when I was a baby.

My parents thought it made me smart.

People visited our town. They bought **fossils**. My family sold fossils for money.

My father died. We needed more money.

What do you know about fossils?

Searching for fossils was not safe.

Falling rocks could have hurt us.

My brother dug up a big **skull**! That was in 1811.

I found the rest of the animal's bones.

The skeleton made people wonder about past life on Earth.

Scientists wanted more fossils.

What do you wonder about?

I was poor. I was a woman.

Scientists didn't respect me. They took my work. They said it was theirs.

How would you feel if
someone took your work?

I read as much as I could. I worked hard to dig up more bones.

I found **fossilized** poop. It told us what **ancient** animals ate.

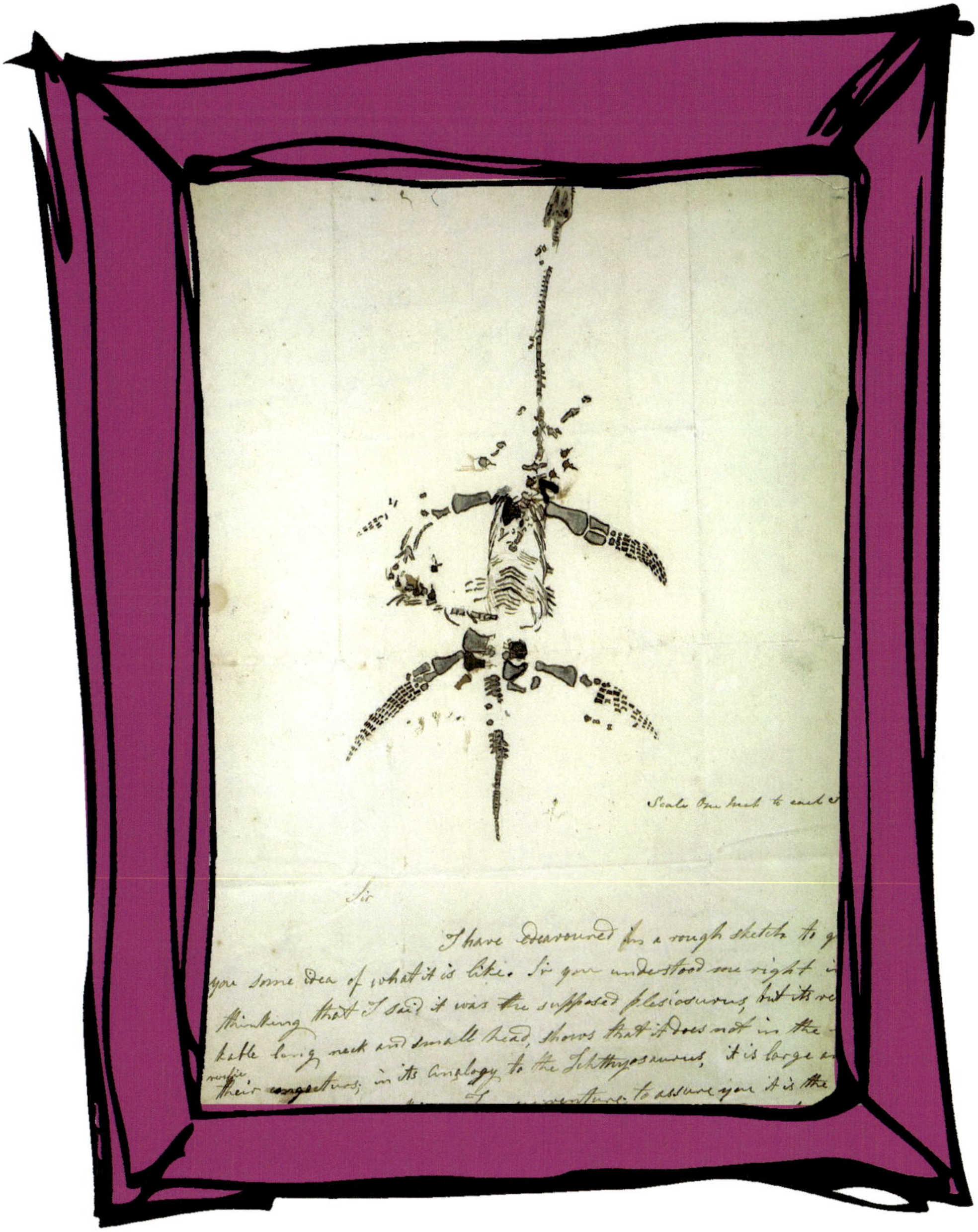

Scale One Inch to each

Sir

I have endeavoured for a rough sketch to g

you some idea of what it is like. Sir you understood me right i

thinking that I said it was the supposed plesiosaurus, but its re

kable long neck and small head, shows that it does not in the

their conjectures; in its analogy to the Ichthyosaurus, it is large a

I venture to assure you it is the

I got sick. I died in 1847.

But my story lives on. Girls can be scientists too!

What would you like to ask me?

1811

1790

Born
1799

1828

1890

Died 1847

glossary

ancient (AYN-shuhnt) very old

fossilized (FAH-suhl-ized) to be changed into a fossil

fossils (FAH-suhlz) bones, shells, or other traces of an animal or plant from millions of years ago, in the form of rocks

lightning (LITE-ning) a flash of light in the sky when there is a storm

scientists (SYE-uhn-tists) people who study nature and the physical world by watching and testing

skull (SKUHL) the bone in the head that protects the brain

index